Learn Node.js

Practical Guide

A. De Quattro

Copyright © 2024

Guide to Node.js

1.Introduction to Node.js

Node.js is an open-source runtime environment based on JavaScript that allows developers to create highly performant network and server-side applications. Node.js uses a non-blocking I/O model, making it extremely efficient in handling asynchronous input/output operations. This allows it to efficiently handle a large number of concurrent connections, making it a great choice for real-time web applications.

Node.js was created by Ryan Dahl in 2009 with the goal of providing developers with a tool to build fast and scalable web applications. Thanks to the Google Chrome V8 JavaScript engine, Node.js offers very high execution performance, allowing developers to write highly performant JavaScript code.

One of the key advantages of Node.js is its ability to efficiently handle asynchronous connections through the use of events and callbacks. This allows developers to write code that can handle many operations simultaneously without blocking the main thread. This non-blocking programming model makes Node.js extremely fast and responsive, ideal for real-time and high-performance web applications.

Node.js is also extremely flexible, with a vast ecosystem of npm modules that allow developers to extend the basic framework functionalities and develop complex applications quickly and easily. This modular approach promotes code reusability and application scalability, allowing developers to focus on business logic rather than low-level operations.

In addition to being used for server-side development, Node.js is also very popular for frontend application development. By using frameworks like Express.js and template engines like Pug, it is possible to create dynamic and responsive user interfaces using JavaScript on both the client and server sides.

In conclusion, Node.js is an extremely powerful and versatile technology that provides developers with the ability to create highly performant and scalable web applications. Thanks to its non-blocking architecture, extreme flexibility, and large community support, Node.js has become one of the most popular frameworks for modern web application development.

2. Installation of Node.js

Node.js is an open-source runtime environment that allows you to run JavaScript on the server side. With Node.js, you can create highly performant and scalable web applications using JavaScript on both the client and server sides. In this article, I will guide you through the process of installing Node.js on your operating system.

Before we begin, it is important to note that Node.js is compatible with various platforms, including Windows, macOS, and Linux. Make sure to download the correct version for your operating system before proceeding with the installation.

Step 1: Download Node.js

The first step to install Node.js on your computer is to download the installation package from the project's official page (https://nodejs.org/). Once you reach the website homepage, you will need to click on the download button to download the latest stable version of Node.js.

If you are using Windows, you will need to download the executable file with the ".msi" extension. For macOS users, it is recommended to download the file with the ".pkg" extension. Finally, if you are using Linux, you will need to follow the specific instructions for your distribution.

Step 2: Install Node.js

Once the download is complete, run the installation package by double-clicking on the executable file. During the installation process, you will need to follow the on-screen instructions and accept the license terms.

While installing Node.js, you can choose the default installation directory or specify a custom one. Make sure to select additional options like npm (Node Package Manager) and Chocolatey (for Windows users) as well.

If everything is successful, you should receive a notification confirming that the installation has been completed successfully. At this point, you can verify that Node.js has been installed correctly by running the following commands from the command line:

```
node -v

npm -v
```

If the commands return the correct version of Node.js and npm, it means the installation was successful.

Step 3: Update Node.js

It is important to keep Node.js always updated to benefit from the latest bug fixes and new features introduced with new versions. To update Node.js, you can use npm, which is installed along with Node.js.

To update Node.js using npm, simply run the following command from the command line:

```
npm install -g n
```

Once the npm installation process is complete, you can update Node.js using the following command:

```
n stable
```

Alternatively, you can specify a specific version of Node.js to install using the following command:

```
n [version]
```

Step 4: Install npm modules

Another important feature of Node.js is its extensive library of npm modules that allow you to extend the basic functionalities of the runtime environment. Installing an npm module is straightforward: just run the following command from the command line:

```
npm install [module_name]
```

Where `[module_name]` represents the name of the npm module to install. For example, if you wanted to install the "express" module, you would simply run the following command:

```
npm install express
```

Once the npm module installation is complete, you can use it within your Node.js applications by including it with the `require()` command.

Step 5: Create a new Node.js application

To conclude this Node.js installation guide, let's see how to create a new Node.js application and run it on your system. First, create a new project folder and navigate to it using the terminal.

Next, run the following command from the command line to initialize a new npm project within the folder:

```
npm init -y
```

This command will create a `package.json` file within your project folder, which will contain information about the project's dependencies and basic configurations.

At this point, you can create a JavaScript file within the project folder and start writing the code for your Node.js application. For example, create an `app.js` file within the project folder and add the following code:

```javascript
// app.js
const http = require('http');

const hostname = '127.0.0.1';
const port = 3000;

const server = http.createServer((req, res) => {
  res.statusCode = 200;
  res.setHeader('Content-Type', 'text/plain');
  res.end('Hello World
```

```
    ');
  });

  server.listen(port, hostname, () => {
    console.log(`Server running at http://${hostname}:${port}/`);
  });
```

Finally, to run the Node.js application you created, simply run the following command from the command line:

```
node app.js
```

If everything was successful, you should see a

message confirming that the server is running on your computer. Open a web browser and type `http://127.0.0.1:3000/` to view the result of your Node.js application.

Congratulations, you have successfully completed the installation of Node.js on your system and created your first Node.js application! Node.js is a powerful tool that allows you to create scalable and performant web applications using JavaScript. Keep exploring the features and libraries available for Node.js to fully harness its potential.

3. JavaScript Fundamentals in Node.js

JavaScript is a programming language commonly used for web application development. Node.js is a JavaScript-based runtime environment that allows you to run server-side JavaScript code, enabling developers to write code on both the client and server side using the same programming language.

In this article, we will delve into the fundamentals of JavaScript in Node.js and provide some practical examples to illustrate how to use the programming language within a Node.js environment.

Variables and Data Types in JavaScript

JavaScript is a scripting language without static data types, which means variables can hold any type of data and the data type can change during program execution. To declare a variable in JavaScript, we use the keywords "var", "let", or "const" followed by the variable name.

Here are some examples of variable declarations in JavaScript:

```javascript
var number = 10;
let string = "Hello, world!";
const PI = 3.14159;
```

In this case, we have declared three variables: "number" of type integer, "string" of type string, and "PI" of type constant decimal number. It is important to note that variables defined with "var" can be reassigned, variables defined with "let" can be reassigned but not re-declared, and variables defined with "const" are constants and cannot be reassigned or re-declared.

Functions in JavaScript

Functions in JavaScript are objects that allow you to organize code into reusable blocks. To define a function in JavaScript, we use the keyword "function" followed by the function name and function parameters enclosed in parentheses.

Here is an example of defining a function in JavaScript:

```javascript
function sum(a, b) {
  return a + b;
}
```

In this case, we have defined a function called "sum" that takes two parameters "a" and "b" and returns the sum of the two parameters. To call a function in JavaScript, we use the function name followed by the parameter values enclosed in parentheses.

```javascript
var result = sum(5, 3);
console.log(result); // Output: 8
```

Objects in JavaScript

Objects in JavaScript are collections of key-value pairs, similar to associative arrays in other programming languages. To create an object in JavaScript, we use curly braces {} and define the object properties and values inside the curly braces.

Here is an example of defining an object in

JavaScript:

```javascript
var person = {
  name: "Mario",
  age: 30,
  profession: "Developer"
};
```

In this case, we have defined an object named "person" with three properties: "name", "age", and "profession". We can access object properties in JavaScript using dot notation or square bracket notation.

```javascript
console.log(person.name); // Output: Mario
```

```
console.log(person["age"]); // Output: 30
```

Arrays in JavaScript

Arrays in JavaScript are objects that allow you to store multiple values in a single variable. To create an array in JavaScript, we use square brackets [] and insert the array values separated by commas.

Here is an example of defining an array in JavaScript:

```javascript
var numbers = [1, 2, 3, 4, 5];
```

We can access array elements in JavaScript using square brackets [] and specifying the index of the element we want to access.

```javascript
console.log(numbers[0]); // Output: 1
console.log(numbers[2]); // Output: 3
```

Loops in JavaScript

Loops in JavaScript allow you to repeatedly execute a block of code until a specified condition is true. The most common loops in JavaScript are the "for" loop, the "while" loop, and the "do-while" loop.

Here are some examples of loops in JavaScript:

For loop:

```javascript
```

```javascript
for(var i = 0; i < 5; i++) {
  console.log(i);
}
```

While loop:

```javascript
var i = 0;
while(i < 5) {
  console.log(i);
  i++;
}
```

Do-while loop:

```javascript
var i = 0;
do {
  console.log(i);
  i++;
} while(i < 5);
```

These are just some of the JavaScript fundamentals you need to know to work with Node.js. Now let's move on to some practical examples that demonstrate how to use JavaScript in Node.js to create server-side applications.

Example 1: Creating an HTTP Server in Node.js

One of the most common ways to use Node.js is to create an HTTP server that can respond to client requests. To create an HTTP server in

Node.js, we use the built-in "http" module of Node.js and define a callback function that will be executed whenever the server receives a new request.

Here is an example of creating an HTTP server in Node.js:

```javascript
const http = require('http');

const server = http.createServer((req, res) => {
  res.statusCode = 200;
  res.setHeader('Content-Type', 'text/plain');
  res.end('Hello, world!');
});

server.listen(3000, 'localhost', () => {
```

```
  console.log('Server running at http://localhost:3000/');

});
```

In this case, we have created an HTTP server that responds with the message "Hello, world!" to all client requests. Using Node.js's built-in "http" module, we are able to create an HTTP server and efficiently handle client requests.

Example 2: Reading a File in Node.js

Another common operation in Node.js is reading files from the local file system. To read a file in Node.js, we use the built-in "fs" module of Node.js and the "fs.readFileSync" function to synchronously read the contents of a file.

Here is an example of reading a file in

Node.js:

```javascript
const fs = require('fs');

const content = fs.readFileSync('file.txt', 'utf-8');

console.log(content);
```

In this case, we are synchronously reading the content of the file "file.txt" and printing it to the console. Using Node.js's "fs" module, we are able to read files from the local file system and manipulate their contents as desired.

Example 3: Creating a Module in Node.js

Node.js allows you to create reusable modules

that can be distributed and used in multiple parts of an application. To create a module in Node.js, we define a function or object and export it using the "module.exports" keyword.

Here is an example of creating a module in Node.js:

```javascript
// module.js
function sum(a, b) {
  return a + b;
}

module.exports = {
  sum: sum
};
```

In this module, we have defined a "sum" function that takes two parameters and returns the sum of the two parameters. By using the "module.exports" keyword, we export the "sum" function so that it can be used in other files within a Node.js application.

By using JavaScript in Node.js, you can create advanced server-side applications and develop reusable modules that can be distributed and used in multiple parts of an application. With a good understanding of JavaScript and Node.js, you can create efficient and scalable web applications that meet the needs of the modern software development world.

4.Modules and Packages in Node.js

Node.js is a JavaScript runtime environment based on Google Chrome's V8 JavaScript engine. Thanks to its event-driven and non-blocking architecture, Node.js has gained popularity for its efficiency and scalability in handling real-time web applications.

A fundamental aspect of Node.js is its handling of modules and packages. Modules in Node.js are individual units of code that can be reused within a project. Every JavaScript file in Node.js is considered a module, which exports its functionalities through the `module.exports` object. This modular programming paradigm allows for organizing code in a modular way, facilitating maintenance and collaboration among developers.

On the other hand, a package is a collection of modules that can be installed through

Node.js's package manager, npm. Packages are distributed through the npm registry, which hosts thousands of open source packages ready to be used within Node.js projects.

The modular approach of Node.js and the package ecosystem provided by npm are essential for developing scalable and maintainable applications. In this article, we will explore in detail how to use modules and packages in Node.js to improve code organization, dependency management, and application development speed.

Modules in Node.js

In Node.js, every JavaScript file is considered a separate module. This means that the code in each file is isolated and only has access to variables and functions defined within that file, unless explicitly exported through `module.exports`.

For example, suppose we have a file `math.js` with the following functions to perform mathematical operations:

```javascript
// math.js

function add(a, b) {
  return a + b;
}

function subtract(a, b) {
  return a - b;
}

module.exports = {
  add,
```

```
  subtract
};
```

In this `math.js` module, we have defined two functions `add` and `subtract`, and exported them using `module.exports`. This allows other modules to import and use these functions within their own files.

To import a module into another JavaScript file, we can use the `require` function. For example, if we want to use the `math.js` module within an `index.js` file, we can do the following:

```javascript
// index.js

const math = require('./math');
```

```js
console.log(math.add(2, 3)); // Output: 5
console.log(math.subtract(5, 3)); // Output: 2
```

In the `index.js` file, we have imported the `math.js` module using the `require` function, which will return the object exported by `math.js`. We can then invoke the `add` and `subtract` functions of the `math.js` module within `index.js`.

Core Modules

In addition to custom modules, Node.js also provides a set of core modules, which are modules integrated into the core of Node.js and do not require any additional installation. For example, the `fs` module provides functionalities for file system input/output operations, while the `http` module allows for creating HTTP servers.

To use a core module in Node.js, we can import it using the `require` function. For example, if we want to use the `fs` module to read a file, we can do so as follows:

```javascript
const fs = require('fs');

fs.readFile('file.txt', 'utf8', (err, data) => {
  if (err) {
    console.error(err);
    return;
  }

  console.log(data);
});
```

```

In the above example, we imported the `fs` module and used the `fs.readFile` function to read the contents of a file named `file.txt`. Once the data is read, we print it to the console. This is just one of the many core modules provided by Node.js to simplify application development.

### Third-Party Modules

In addition to custom and core modules, Node.js also supports the use of third-party modules. These modules are packages published on the npm registry and can be easily installed using Node.js's package manager, npm.

To install a third-party module, we can use the `npm install` command. For example, if we want to install the `lodash` module, a popular
```

JavaScript library for manipulating arrays and objects, we can do so as follows:

```
npm install lodash
```

Once a third-party module is installed, we can use it in our Node.js projects just like custom and core modules. For example, if we want to use the `chunk` function from `lodash` to split an array into smaller parts, we can do so as follows:

```javascript
const _ = require('lodash');

const chunkedArray = _.chunk([1, 2, 3, 4, 5], 2);
console.log(chunkedArray); // Output: [[1, 2],
```

[3, 4], [5]]
```

In this example, we imported the `lodash` module with the name `_` and used the `_.chunk` function to split an array into smaller parts of two elements each. This is just one of the many third-party modules available on npm to simplify Node.js application development.

## Packages in Node.js

Packages are a fundamental concept in Node.js and refer to a collection of modules that can be easily shared and distributed through the npm registry. Thanks to npm, developers can install, update, and remove packages with ease, improving code modularity and reusability.
```

package.json

Every Node.js project contains a `package.json` file, which serves as a manifesto for the project and stores crucial information such as the project name, version, dependencies, and startup scripts. This file is essential for managing the project's packages and dependencies.

An example of a `package.json` file might look like this:

```json
{
  "name": "my-project",
  "version": "1.0.0",
  "description": "A Node.js project",
  "main": "index.js",
  "scripts": {
```

```
    "start": "node index.js"
  },
  "dependencies": {
    "express": "^4.17.1",
    "lodash": "^4.17.21"
  }
}
```

In this example, the `package.json` file contains information such as the project name, version, a brief description, the main file `index.js`, startup scripts, and the project's dependencies, in this case `express` and `lodash`.

Installing Packages

To install the packages declared in the

`package.json` file, we can run the `npm install` command. This command will read the `package.json` file and install all the dependencies listed in the "dependencies" field.

For example, if we want to install all project dependencies from the `package.json` file, we can run the following command:

```
npm install
```

This command will install all the packages declared in the `package.json` file in the `node_modules` directory. Each package will be saved within the `node_modules` directory, making it easy to manage project dependencies.

Version Management

Dependencies declared in the `package.json` file can include versioning criteria. For example, the dependency of `lodash` in the `package.json` file from the previous example contains the following versioning criteria: `"lodash": "^4.17.21"`. This means that npm will install the latest 4.x.x version of `lodash`, but will not install versions 5.x.x or higher.

More precise versioning criteria can be specified using different operators. For example, the `>=` symbol indicates "greater than or equal to," while the `>` symbol indicates "greater than." Symbols like `~` and `^` can also be used to establish more flexible versioning criteria.

Using Packages

Once packages are installed, we can use them

in our Node.js projects like custom and core modules. For example, if we have installed the `express` package to create a web server, we can do so as follows:

```javascript
const express = require('express');
const app = express();

app.get('/', (req, res) => {
  res.send('Hello, World!');
});

app.listen(3000, () => {
  console.log('Server is running on port 3000');
});
```

In this example, we imported the `express` package, created an instance of an Express application, and defined a route that returns the message "Hello, World!" when accessing the root of the server. Finally, we started the server on a specific port.

Global Packages

In addition to local packages installed within a Node.js project, it is possible to install global packages that are available system-wide. These packages are useful for tools and utilities that need to be accessible in all Node.js projects on the system.

To install a package globally, we can use the `npm install -g` command. For example, if we want to install the `nodemon` package globally to automatically restart the Node.js server after saving changes to the code, we can do so as follows:

```
npm install -g nodemon
```

Once a package is installed globally, we can use it throughout the system by running its command from any Node.js project without having to install it locally.

Modules and packages are fundamental elements in the world of Node.js and are essential for creating scalable, modular, and maintainable applications. Through Node.js's modular programming and npm's package ecosystem, developers can easily manage code, dependencies, and feature reuse efficiently.

By using custom modules, core modules, and third-party modules, developers can organize code into functional units, improving code readability and maintainability. Additionally, by installing and managing packages through npm, external features can be easily added to Node.js projects, making them more powerful and versatile.

In conclusion, the use of modules and packages in Node.js is essential for improving productivity, collaboration, and scalability of modern web applications. By fully leveraging this powerful dependency management system, developers can build superior-quality applications more efficiently and effectively.

5. Error Handling in Node.js

Errors are an inevitable aspect of developing any software project, including those developed in Node.js. It is important to properly handle errors to ensure that the application is robust, reliable, and able to provide an optimal user experience. In this article, we will explore the main approaches to error handling in Node.js and provide some practical examples to illustrate how to handle different types of errors.

Handling Synchronous Errors in Node.js

In Node.js, synchronous errors are errors that occur during the execution of blocking or synchronous operations, such as accessing files or performing complex mathematical operations. To handle synchronous errors, you can use the try-catch block. For example, consider the following code that attempts to access a file that may not exist:

```javascript
const fs = require('fs');

try {
  const data = fs.readFileSync('file.txt', 'utf8');
  console.log(data);
} catch (error) {
  console.error('Error while retrieving data from file:', error);
}
```

In this example, the try-catch block is used to handle the error that may occur while reading the 'file.txt' file. If an error occurs, an error message with the description of the error will be printed. It is important to note that the try-catch block only captures synchronous errors and is not able to handle asynchronous errors, which are errors that occur during the execution of asynchronous operations such as external API calls or non-blocking I/O operations.

Handling Asynchronous Errors in Node.js

To handle asynchronous errors in Node.js, you can use callback functions or promises. For example, consider the following code, where a callback function is used to handle the error during an asynchronous call to an API:

```javascript
const axios = require('axios');

axios.get('https://api.example.com/data')
  .then(response => {
    console.log(response.data);
  })
```

```
  .catch(error => {

    console.error('Error during API call:', error);

  });
```

In this example, the axios.get() function makes an asynchronous call to the 'https://api.example.com/data' API. The call will return a promise that will be resolved with the response data if the call is successful, or rejected with an error if an issue occurs during the call. You can use the catch() method to handle the error if the API call is not successful.

Alternatively, you can use promises to handle errors more concisely and readably. For example, the following code uses a promise to handle the error while reading a file:

```javascript
const fs = require('fs').promises;

fs.readFile('file.txt', 'utf8')
  .then(data => {
    console.log(data);
  })
  .catch(error => {
    console.error('Error while reading the file:', error);
  });
```

In this example, the fs.readFile() method will return a promise that will be resolved with the file data if the read is successful, or rejected with an error if an issue occurs during the file read. You can use the catch() method to handle the error if the file read is not successful.

Handling Uncaught Errors in Node.js

It is important to properly handle all errors that occur in Node.js code to ensure that the application is stable and reliable. However, there may be cases where errors occur that are not explicitly handled by the code. In such cases, Node.js provides a default handler for uncaught errors, which involves setting a listener for the 'uncaughtException' event on the process object. For example, consider the following code that sets a handler for uncaught errors:

```javascript
process.on('uncaughtException', error => {
  console.error('Uncaught error:', error);
  process.exit(1);
});
```

```
// Simulating an uncaught error
throw new Error('Uncaught error');
```

In this example, we have defined a listener for the 'uncaughtException' event on the process object that handles uncaught errors and prints an error message with the description of the error. Additionally, you can call the process.exit() method to terminate the application execution with a non-zero exit code.

However, it is important to note that handling uncaught errors through the 'uncaughtException' event is not considered a best practice, as it could lead to unexpected behaviors and data loss. Instead, it is advisable to implement global error handling wrappers to safely and robustly capture and log unhandled errors.

Implementing an Error Handling Wrapper in Node.js

To implement an error handling wrapper in Node.js, you can use an Express middleware to capture and handle errors coming from HTTP requests. For example, consider the following Express middleware that captures and handles errors from HTTP requests:

```javascript
const express = require('express');
const app = express();

// Middleware to capture errors
app.use((error, req, res, next) => {
  console.error('Error during request handling:', error);
  res.status(500).send('Internal server error');
});
```

```
// Application routes
app.get('/', (req, res) => {
  throw new Error('Error processing request');
});

// Starting the server
app.listen(3000, () => {
  console.log('Server listening on port 3000');
});
```

In this example, we have defined an Express middleware that captures errors during the handling of HTTP requests and directs them to the error handling middleware. If an error occurs during the processing of a request, an exception will be thrown to simulate an internal server error. The error handling middleware prints an error message with the description of the error and returns an HTTP response with a status of 500.

Conclusion

Error handling is a fundamental aspect of software development in Node.js. It is important to know how to properly handle synchronous and asynchronous errors to ensure that the application is robust, reliable, and able to provide an optimal user experience. Additionally, it is important to implement global error handling wrappers to capture and log unhandled errors safely and robustly. With proper error handling, you can improve the quality and stability of the application, and ensure a seamless user experience.

6.Events and callbacks in Node.js

Node.js is a very powerful framework for developing server-side applications. One of the key features of Node.js is event and callback management. In this article, we will explore what events and callbacks are in Node.js and how to use them effectively.

Events in Node.js are situations that occur within a Node application, such as reading a file, an incoming HTTP request, or a mouse click. Events are emitted by objects called "emitters" and can be captured and handled by functions called "listeners". When an event is emitted, all associated listeners are executed.

To use events in Node.js, you need to use the built-in "events" module of Node.js. This module provides an interface for event management and allows you to create your own emitters and listeners. Here is an example of how to use events in Node.js:

```javascript
const EventEmitter = require('events');

// Create a custom emitter
const myEmitter = new EventEmitter();

// Define a listener for the 'greeting' event
myEmitter.on('greeting', () => {
  console.log('Hello world!');
});

// Emit the 'greeting' event
myEmitter.emit('greeting');
```

In this example, we create a custom emitter

called "myEmitter" and define a listener for the 'greeting' event. When the 'greeting' event is emitted, the listener associated with this event is executed and prints out "Hello world!" to the console.

Callbacks, on the other hand, are functions that are passed as arguments to other functions and are executed once the operation is completed. Callbacks are essential in Node.js because Node.js is based on an asynchronous and non-blocking model. This means that operations are executed asynchronously, allowing code execution to continue without waiting for the completion of operations.

Callbacks are often used in Node.js to handle operations such as reading files, HTTP requests, or database queries. An example of using callbacks in Node.js is as follows:

```javascript
```

```js
const fs = require('fs');

// Read the content of a file asynchronously
fs.readFile('file.txt', 'utf8', (err, data) => {
  if (err) throw err;
  console.log(data);
});
```

In this example, we use the fs module's readFile function to read the content of a file asynchronously. We pass three arguments to the readFile method: the name of the file to read, the file format (in this case 'utf8' to read the file as a string), and a callback that is executed once the file reading operation is completed. If an error occurs during the file reading, the callback will receive the error as the first argument.

Callbacks are also capable of handling complex asynchronous situations, such as database queries or incoming HTTP requests. When performing a database query or making an HTTP request in Node.js, a callback is often used to handle the response from the database or server.

Another interesting feature of Node.js is the ability to use callback hell or "callback hell". This occurs when deeply nested callbacks are used, making the code difficult to read and maintain. To avoid callback hell, you can use promises or async/await.

Promises are another form of handling asynchronous operations in Node.js. Promises are objects that represent the completion or failure of an asynchronous operation and allow you to write code in a more readable and maintainable way than callbacks.

Here is an example of how to use promises in

Node.js:

```javascript
const fs = require('fs').promises;

// Read the content of a file asynchronously using promises
fs.readFile('file.txt', 'utf8')
  .then(data => {
    console.log(data);
  })
  .catch(err => {
    console.error(err);
  });
```

In this example, we use the fs.promises.readFile method to read the content of a file asynchronously using promises. When the file is successfully read, the promise is resolved and the function passed to then is executed. If an error occurs, the promise is rejected and the function passed to catch is executed.

Another alternative to callbacks and promises is to use async/await. Async/await is a feature of ES6 that allows you to write asynchronous code in a synchronous and readable way. Here is an example of how to use async/await in Node.js:

```javascript
const fs = require('fs').promises;

// Asynchronous function to read the content of a file
async function readFile() {
  try {
```

```
    const data = await fs.readFile('file.txt', 'utf8');
    console.log(data);
  } catch (err) {
    console.error(err);
  }
}

// Call the asynchronous function
readFile();
```

In this example, we define an asynchronous function called "readFile" that uses the await expression to read the content of a file asynchronously. The code inside the asynchronous function is executed synchronously, making the code more readable.

Events and callbacks are fundamental concepts in Node.js that allow you to handle asynchronous operations effectively. We can use events to handle situations that occur within a Node application, while callbacks allow us to handle asynchronous operations such as reading files, database queries, or HTTP requests. Promises and async/await are alternatives to callbacks that allow you to write more readable and maintainable asynchronous code. Knowing how to use events and callbacks in Node.js is essential for effective and scalable server-side application development.

7.Creating a web server with Node.js

Creating a web server with Node.js is a very common practice in the world of web development, as Node.js offers a highly performant and scalable server-side environment. In this article, I will describe step by step how to create a basic web server using Node.js, and provide some code examples to illustrate the key concepts.

Step 1: Installing Node.js

Before being able to create a web server with Node.js, it is necessary to install Node.js on your computer. Node.js can be downloaded from the official website (https://nodejs.org/) and follow the installation instructions for your operating system.

Step 2: Creating a JavaScript file for the server

Once Node.js is installed, you can create a

JavaScript file that will contain the code for the web server. We will use the `http` module of Node.js to create the server and handle incoming HTTP requests.

Here is an example of code for a very simple web server that returns a "Hello, world!" message:

```javascript
// Import the http module of Node.js
const http = require('http');

// Create the server
const server = http.createServer((req, res) => {
  res.writeHead(200, { 'Content-Type': 'text/plain' });
  res.end('Hello, world!');
});
```

```
// Start the server on port 3000
server.listen(3000, () => {
  console.log('Server running on http://localhost:3000');
});
```

Save this code in a file named `server.js`.

Step 3: Starting the server

To start the server, open the terminal and navigate to the directory where the `server.js` file is located. Then run the command `node server.js`. The server will start and can be accessed through the browser at the address `http://localhost:3000`.

Step 4: Handling routes

To make the server more dynamic and handle different HTTP requests differently, you can use the `url` module of Node.js to parse the request URL and handle the corresponding routes.

Here is an example of code to handle two different routes on the server:

```javascript
const http = require('http');
const url = require('url');

const server = http.createServer((req, res) => {
  const parsedUrl = url.parse(req.url, true);

  if (parsedUrl.pathname === '/hello') {
    res.writeHead(200, { 'Content-Type': 'text/plain' });
```

```
    res.end('Hello, world!');

  } else if (parsedUrl.pathname ===
'/goodbye') {

    res.writeHead(200, { 'Content-Type':
'text/plain' });

    res.end('Goodbye, world!');

  } else {

    res.writeHead(404, { 'Content-Type':
'text/plain' });

    res.end('404 Not Found');

  }
});


server.listen(3000, () => {

  console.log('Server running on
http://localhost:3000');

});
```

In this example, the server handles two different routes: `/hello` and `/goodbye`. If the request URL matches one of these two routes, the server will return the corresponding message. Otherwise, a 404 error message will be returned.

Step 5: Using a framework for route handling

To handle routes in a more structured and modular way, you can use a Node.js framework like Express.js. Express.js simplifies the creation of complex web servers and offers a wide range of additional features.

Here is an example of how to use Express.js to handle routes on a web server:

```javascript
const express = require('express');
const app = express();
```

```
app.get('/hello', (req, res) => {
  res.send('Hello, world!');
});

app.get('/goodbye', (req, res) => {
  res.send('Goodbye, world!');
});

app.use((req, res) => {
  res.status(404).send('404 Not Found');
});

app.listen(3000, () => {
  console.log('Server running on http://localhost:3000');
});
```

```

In this example, the routes `/hello` and `/goodbye` are defined using the `app.get()` method of Express.js. Additionally, a fallback route has been defined to handle requests for non-existent routes.

By using Express.js, you can create more complex web servers and handle requests more efficiently and organizedly.

In conclusion, creating a web server with Node.js is a relatively simple and powerful process. With Node.js, it is possible to create highly performant and scalable web servers, thanks to its event-driven asynchronous architecture. Using the `http` and `url` modules of Node.js, basic web servers can be created, and by using frameworks like Express.js, more structured and modular web servers can be created.
```

8. Managing HTTP requests with Node.js (GET and POST) HTML Template for Node.js

Managing HTTP requests with Node.js is a fundamental process for creating web applications. Node.js is a platform that allows the execution of server-side JavaScript code, enabling efficient and flexible handling of HTTP requests.

In managing HTTP requests with Node.js, requests can be of two main types: GET and POST. GET requests are used to retrieve data from the server, while POST requests are used to send data to the server. These two types of requests can be handled through Node.js using the built-in APIs provided by the "http" module.

To handle GET and POST requests with Node.js, we can use the following example code:

```javascript
const http = require('http');

const server = http.createServer((req, res) => {
  if (req.method === 'GET') {
    res.writeHead(200, {'Content-Type': 'text/plain'});
    res.end('GET request received');
  } else if (req.method === 'POST') {
    res.writeHead(200, {'Content-Type': 'text/plain'});
    res.end('POST request received');
  } else {
    res.writeHead(405, {'Content-Type': 'text/plain'});
    res.end('Method not allowed');
  }
```

```
});


server.listen(3000, () => {
  console.log('Server running on port 3000');
});
```

In this code example, we create an HTTP server using the "http" module of Node.js. We use the "createServer" method to create the server and handle incoming requests. Inside the callback function passed to "createServer", we check the request method (req.method) and return a different response based on the type of request (GET or POST).

In addition to managing HTTP requests with Node.js, we can also use HTML templates to generate dynamic web pages. One way to do this is by using the "ejs" (Embedded JavaScript) module, which allows us to embed

JavaScript directly within our HTML files.

Here is an example of how to use the "ejs" module to create an HTML template with Node.js:

1. Install the "ejs" module using npm:

```
npm install ejs
```

2. Create an HTML file with the extension ".ejs" that will use the template:

```html
<!DOCTYPE html>
<html>
```

```
<head>
  <title><%= title %></title>
</head>
<body>
  <h1><%= message %></h1>
</body>
</html>
```

3. Use the "ejs" module in our Node.js server to render the template:

```javascript
const http = require('http');
const ejs = require('ejs');
const fs = require('fs');
```

```javascript
const server = http.createServer((req, res) => {
  fs.readFile('template.ejs', 'utf8', (err, data) => {
    if (err) {
      res.writeHead(500, {'Content-Type': 'text/plain'});
      res.end('Internal Server Error');
    } else {
      const html = ejs.render(data, {title: 'Sample Page', message: 'Hello World!'});
      res.writeHead(200, {'Content-Type': 'text/html'});
      res.end(html);
    }
  });
});

server.listen(3000, () => {
```

```
  console.log('Server running on port 3000');
});
```

In this example, we use the "fs" module of Node.js to read the content of the "template.ejs" file, which contains our HTML template. We use the "render" method of the "ejs" module to render the template and pass the necessary data to successfully render the template.

This way, we can create dynamic web pages using HTML templates with Node.js and the "ejs" module.

In addition to managing HTTP requests and using HTML templates, we can also use the "bind" module of Node.js to link functions to a specific context, ensuring that they maintain the same execution context in which they were defined.

Here is an example of how to use the "bind" method to maintain the context of a function in Node.js:

```javascript
const person = {
  name: 'Alice',
  greet: function() {
    console.log(`Hello, ${this.name}!`);
  }
};

const greetAlice = person.greet.bind(person);
greetAlice(); // Output: Hello, Alice!
```

In the code example above, we define an

object "person" with a "name" property and a "greet" method that prints a greeting using the object's name. We use the "bind" method to link the "greet" function to the "person" object and maintain the execution context of the function.

This is just an example of how to use the "bind" method in Node.js to maintain the execution context of a function. We can use the "bind" method in various situations where it is important to maintain the context of a function, for example, when defining callbacks to handle HTTP requests.

In conclusion, managing HTTP requests with Node.js is essential for creating efficient and flexible web applications. We can use HTML templates to generate dynamic web pages, and the "bind" module to maintain the execution context of a function. With these tools at our disposal, we can create powerful and performant web applications using Node.js.

9. Creating APIs with Node.js

Creating APIs with Node.js is a fundamental task for developing modern and high-performance web applications. APIs (Application Programming Interfaces) allow different parts of an application to communicate with each other efficiently and securely, enabling developers to integrate functionalities and data from various sources.

Node.js is a Javascript runtime environment based on Chrome V8 that allows running Javascript code on the server-side. Due to its speed and efficiency, Node.js has become one of the most popular development environments for creating web applications and RESTful APIs.

To create an API with Node.js, you can use various frameworks and libraries such as Express.js, Koa.js, Hapi.js, and many others. In this article, we will see how to create a

RESTful API using Express.js, one of the most popular frameworks for web application development with Node.js.

To begin, make sure you have Node.js installed on your system. Next, create a new folder for your project and open a terminal within it. Run the following command to initialize your Node.js project:

```
npm init -y
```

This command will create a `package.json` file with basic configurations for your project. Next, install the Express.js framework by running the command:

```
```

```
npm install express
```

Express.js is a lightweight and flexible framework that simplifies the creation of web servers and RESTful APIs. Once Express.js is installed, create a new file called `app.js` and start configuring your Express server.

```javascript
// Import the Express module
const express = require('express');
// Create an Express application
const app = express();
// Define a basic route
app.get('/', (req, res) => {
  res.send('Welcome to our API!');
});
```

```
// Start the server on port 3000
app.listen(3000, () => {
  console.log('Server is listening on port 3000');
});
```

In this code, we have imported the Express module, created an Express application, and defined a basic route that returns a welcome message when accessing the root of the server. Finally, we have started the server on port 3000 and printed a confirmation message on the console.

To run our Express server, we can use the command:

```
node app.js
```

```

Once the server is up and running, we can access our API at `http://localhost:3000` and see the welcome message.

Now that our Express server is running, we can start defining our RESTful APIs to handle client requests. For example, we can create a route to retrieve a list of users and a route to add a new user to the system.

```javascript
// List of users
let users = [
   { id: 1, name: 'Alice' },
   { id: 2, name: 'Bob' },
   { id: 3, name: 'Charlie' }
];

```
// Route to get the list of users
app.get('/users', (req, res) => {
  res.json(users);
});

// Route to add a new user
app.post('/users', (req, res) => {
  const newUser = req.body;
  users.push(newUser);
  res.status(201).json(newUser);
});
```

In this code, we have defined a `users` variable that contains a list of sample users. We then created two Express routes: a `GET` route to retrieve the list of users and a `POST` route to add a new user to the system. The `POST` route receives the new user from the request body and adds it to the list of users, returning the new user with a status of 201 Created.

To access the request body of the POST request, you need to install the `body-parser` middleware, which allows parsing data sent in the body of the HTTP request. Install the body-parser middleware by running the command:

```
npm install body-parser
```

Next, configure our Express server to use the body-parser middleware in the `app.js` file:

```javascript
```

```js
// Import the body-parser module
const bodyParser = require('body-parser');
// Configure body-parser to parse request bodies as JSON
app.use(bodyParser.json());
```

Once the body-parser middleware is configured, we can now send POST requests to our Express server to add new users to the list. For example, we can use a tool like Postman to send a POST request to `http://localhost:3000/users` with the new user in the request body in JSON format:

```json
{
  "id": 4,
  "name": "David"
}
```

```

After sending the request, the server will respond with the new user added to the list of users and the status 201 Created.

In addition to basic CRUD (Create, Read, Update, Delete) operations, you can implement other advanced functionalities in RESTful APIs using Express.js. For example, you can handle authentication and authorization, configure middleware for error handling, create endpoints for file downloads, and much more.

An important aspect of creating APIs with Node.js is the management of configuration files and environment variables. You can use the `dotenv` module to load environment variables from a `.env` file and use them within your Node.js project securely and flexibly.
```

Install the `dotenv` module by running the command:

```
npm install dotenv
```

Next, create a `.env` file in the root of your project and add the necessary environment variables, for example:

```
PORT=3000
DB_URL=mongodb://localhost:27017/mydatabase
```

Finally, use the `dotenv` module to load the environment variables in our `app.js` project:

```javascript
require('dotenv').config();

const port = process.env.PORT || 3000;
const dbUrl = process.env.DB_URL;

app.listen(port, () => {
  console.log(`Server is listening on port ${port}`);
});
```

By using `dotenv`, environment variables can be easily managed and updated without directly modifying the source code, ensuring greater flexibility and security in API deployment.

In conclusion, creating APIs with Node.js and Express.js is an intuitive and powerful process that allows developers to create high-performance and scalable web applications. By using concepts such as routing, middleware, and Node.js modules, you can create efficient and secure RESTful APIs to meet the complex needs of modern web applications.

Finally, there are many other aspects to consider when creating APIs with Node.js, such as handling authorizations and authentications, API documentation, testing, and performance monitoring. With a solid understanding of Node.js and Express.js, you can create powerful and customizable APIs for any type of web application.

10. Database Connectivity with Node.js

When talking about database connectivity with Node.js, it refers to the ability of Node.js to interact with a database to store, retrieve, and manipulate data. This functionality is essential for many types of web applications and allows for efficient and secure data management within an application.

Node.js is a JavaScript runtime environment that allows for running JavaScript code on the server side. With Node.js, you can create web servers, process HTTP requests, manage events, and much more. To connect to a database with Node.js, you need to use a connectivity module that provides the necessary functionality to interact with the chosen database.

There are several database connectivity modules available for Node.js, with the most popular ones being `mongodb`, `mysql`, `sequelize`, `mongodb-client`, `mongoose`, `pg`, `sqlite3`, just to name a few. Each module offers specific functionality for the type of database you want to interact with, whether it is a relational database like MySQL or PostgreSQL, or a NoSQL database like MongoDB.

Below, we will see how to connect to a MySQL database using the `mysql` module and a MongoDB database using the `mongodb` module. Let's start with an example of connecting to a MySQL database.

To connect to a MySQL database with Node.js, you need to first install the `mysql` module using npm, Node.js's package manager. Here's how to do it:

```bash
npm install mysql
```

Once the `mysql` module is installed, you can use it to connect to a MySQL database and interact with it using SQL queries. Here is an example of code that connects Node.js to a MySQL database and selects all records from a table called `users`:

```javascript
const mysql = require('mysql');

// Create a connection to the database
const connection = mysql.createConnection({
  host: 'localhost',
  user: 'root',
  password: 'password',
  database: 'mydatabase'
});
```

```javascript
// Connect to the database
connection.connect();

// Query to select all records from the users table
connection.query('SELECT * FROM users', (error, results, fields) => {
  if (error) throw error;
  console.log('The records in the users table are: ', results);
});

// Close the database connection
connection.end();
```

In this example, the code creates a connection to the MySQL database by specifying the host, user, password, and database name. It then executes a query to select all records from the `users` table and prints the results to the console. Finally, it closes the database connection.

Now let's see an example of connecting to a MongoDB database using the `mongodb` module. Again, you need to install the module using npm:

```bash
npm install mongodb
```

Once the `mongodb` module is installed, you can use it to connect to a MongoDB database and interact with it using MongoDB queries. Here is an example of code that connects Node.js to a MongoDB database and inserts a new document into a collection called `books`:

```javascript
const MongoClient = require('mongodb').MongoClient;

// MongoDB database connection URL
const url = 'mongodb://localhost:27017';

// Database name
const dbName = 'mydatabase';

// Connect to the database
MongoClient.connect(url, { useNewUrlParser: true, useUnifiedTopology: true }, (error, client) => {
  if (error) throw error;
  console.log('Successfully connected to the database');
```

```javascript
// Select the database
const db = client.db(dbName);

// Insert a new document into the books collection
db.collection('books').insertOne({
    title: 'The Lord of the Rings',
    author: 'J.R.R. Tolkien'
  }, (error, result) => {
    if (error) throw error;
    console.log('New document inserted successfully');
  });

// Close the database connection
client.close();
});
```

```

In this example, the code connects to a MongoDB database by specifying the connection URL and the database name. It then selects the database and inserts a new document into the `books` collection. Finally, it closes the database connection.

In addition to the examples of MySQL and MongoDB database connectivity presented above, there are many other options and configurations available for connecting Node.js to different types of databases. You can also use Object-Relational Mapping (ORM) tools like Sequelize or Mongoose to simplify and automate database operations.

In conclusion, database connectivity with Node.js is a crucial aspect for developing modern and efficient web applications. With the connectivity modules available and the features offered by Node.js, you can create
```

scalable, performant, and secure applications that seamlessly interact with any type of database.

11. Using middleware in Node.js

Middleware in Node.js is a fundamental concept in creating robust and scalable web applications. Middleware is essentially a function that has access to the request object and response object of a Node.js application and can modify these objects or perform specific actions before they are passed to the endpoint handler function. This allows for writing reusable code and cleanly separating responsibilities within a Node.js application.

A common example of middleware in Node.js is logging middleware, which logs the HTTP requests received by the application along with details such as the requested URL, HTTP method used, processing time, and more. This type of middleware is extremely useful for debugging and monitoring application performance.

Another common example of middleware is

authentication middleware, which checks whether a user is authorized to access a specific protected resource of the application. This type of middleware is crucial for ensuring the security of web applications and protecting sensitive user information.

To use middleware in Node.js, you can use the Express framework, one of the most popular and widely used frameworks for creating web applications in Node.js. Express provides a simple and intuitive way to define and use middleware within an application.

Below is an example of how to use logging middleware in an Express application:

```javascript
const express = require('express');
const app = express();
```

```javascript
// Logging middleware
app.use((req, res, next) => {
  console.log(`${new Date().toISOString()} - ${req.method} ${req.url}`);
  next();
});

// Route handler
app.get('/', (req, res) => {
  res.send('Hello World!');
});

app.listen(3000, () => {
  console.log('Server running on port 3000');
});
```

In this example, we have defined a middleware function that logs the current date, HTTP method, and URL of the request received by the Express application before passing it to the endpoint handler function that returns 'Hello World!' as a response.

Multiple middleware can be used in an Express application by specifying multiple middleware functions using the `use()` method of Express. For example, we can add authentication middleware before handling a request:

```javascript
// Authentication middleware
app.use((req, res, next) => {
  if (req.headers['authorization'] === 'secret-token') {
    next();
  } else {
```

```
    res.status(401).send('Unauthorized');
  }
});

// Route handler protected by authentication
app.get('/protected', (req, res) => {
  res.send('Protected route');
});
```

In this example, before handling the request for the '/protected' endpoint, we check if the authorization token is present in the request headers. If the token is correct, the request is passed to the endpoint handler function; otherwise, an HTTP 401 (Unauthorized) status is returned as a response.

Furthermore, Express offers the flexibility to use third-party middleware to extend the functionality of an application. There are many middleware available for Express that can facilitate web application development, such as middleware for session management, data compression, request validation, error handling, and more.

Middleware is a powerful tool for improving modularity, readability, and maintainability of code in a Node.js application. By using middleware in conjunction with a framework like Express, sophisticated and scalable web applications can be efficiently created.

12. Session and Cookie Management in Node.js

Node.js is a JavaScript runtime environment based on Google Chrome's V8 engine that allows you to run JavaScript code outside of the browser. It is widely used for creating server-side applications and RESTful APIs due to its speed and scalability.

Managing sessions and cookies in Node.js is essential for user security and authentication. Sessions are a mechanism for storing state information between HTTP requests, allowing users to maintain their authentication and preferences during their browsing session. Cookies, on the other hand, are small files stored on the client side that contain information such as session IDs or user preferences.

To manage sessions and cookies in Node.js, there are several modules and libraries available that make the process easy and secure. One popular module is express-session, which provides middleware for managing sessions in an Express application. Let's see how to implement session and cookie management in Node.js with a practical example.

Installation of required modules:

Before getting started, make sure you have Node.js installed on your system. You can easily do this by running the command npm install -g node.

Now you can create a Node.js project and install the necessary modules like express and express-session by running the following commands:

```
```

```
npm init -y
npm install express express-session
```

Creating a basic web server:

Once the modules are installed, we can create a basic web server using Express. Let's create a file called server.js and add the following code:

```javascript
const express = require('express');
const session = require('express-session');

const app = express();

app.use(session({
```

```javascript
  secret: 'my-secret-key',
  resave: false,
  saveUninitialized: true
}));

app.get('/', (req, res) => {
  if(req.session.views) {
    req.session.views++;
  } else {
    req.session.views = 1;
  }
  res.send(`You have visited this page ${req.session.views} times`);
});

app.listen(3000, () => {
  console.log('Server running on http://localhost:3000');
```

```
});
```

In this code, we are using the express module to create an instance of an Express application and the express-session module to manage sessions. We configure the session middleware with a secret key and other options like resave and saveUninitialized.

We create a main route '/' that increments a counter every time a user visits the page and displays the number of visits.

Start the server by running the command node server.js and open the browser at http://localhost:3000 to see the result.

Cookie management:

To manage cookies in Node.js, we can use the cookie-parser module along with express. Let's install it by running the command npm install cookie-parser.

Let's modify our server.js code to use cookie-parser:

```javascript
const express = require('express');
const session = require('express-session');
const cookieParser = require('cookie-parser');

const app = express();

app.use(cookieParser());
app.use(session({
  secret: 'my-secret-key',
```

```javascript
  resave: false,
  saveUninitialized: true
}));

app.get('/', (req, res) => {
  if(req.session.views) {
    req.session.views++;
  } else {
    req.session.views = 1;
  }
  res.cookie('my-cookie', '123');
  res.send(`You have visited this page ${req.session.views} times`);
});

app.listen(3000, () => {
  console.log('Server running on http://localhost:3000');
```

```
});
```

In this code, we have added cookie-parser as an application middleware and used the res.cookie() method to set a cookie with the name 'my-cookie' and the value '123' on the HTTP response.

Now when a user visits the page, a cookie with the name my-cookie will be set on the client. You can view the cookies in the browser using the developer tools.

Conclusion:

Session and cookie management in Node.js is essential for ensuring user security and authentication in web applications. By using modules like express-session and cookie-parser, you can easily manage sessions and cookies in Node.js.

In the example above, we created a basic web server using Express and managed sessions and cookies to track user visits. You can extend this logic to implement more complex features like user authentication and session state maintenance.

Always remember to protect sensitive information such as session keys and configure security options properly to prevent attacks like cookie interception.

13. Authorization and authentication management in Node.js

Managing permissions and authentications in Node.js is a fundamental aspect to ensure the security of web applications. In this article, we will explore different techniques and libraries that can be used to implement a robust and secure authentication and authorization system in a Node.js application.

Authentication is the process by which a user proves to be who they say they are, while authorization is the process by which it is determined which actions a user is authorized to perform within the application. These two aspects are crucial to protect the resources of the application and ensure that only authorized users can access certain features or sensitive data.

One of the most common techniques for authentication in Node.js is the use of JSON

Web Tokens (JWT). A JWT is a digitally signed token that contains information about the user and can be used to verify the authenticity of a user. To use JWT in Node.js, you can use the 'jsonwebtoken' library.

Here is an example of how you can generate a JWT in Node.js:

```javascript
const jwt = require('jsonwebtoken');

const payload = {
  user_id: 123456,
  username: 'johndoe'
};

const secretKey = 'mysecretkey';
```

```javascript
const token = jwt.sign(payload, secretKey, { expiresIn: '1h' });

console.log(token);
```

In this example, the `jwt.sign` function is used to generate a JWT from a payload containing user information. The generated token has a validity of 1 hour and is signed using the secret key `mysecretkey`.

Once the JWT is generated, you can use it to authenticate the user in subsequent requests by sending the token in the authorization headers. Here is an example of how you can verify a JWT in Node.js:

```javascript
const jwt = require('jsonwebtoken');
```

```javascript
const secretKey = 'mysecretkey';
const token = 'xxxxxxxxxxxxxxxxxxxxxxxxxxxxxx'; // JWT to be verified

jwt.verify(token, secretKey, (err, decoded) => {
  if (err) {
    console.error('Invalid token');
  } else {
    console.log(decoded);
  }
});
```

In this example, the `jwt.verify` function is used to verify a JWT using the secret key `mysecretkey`. If the token is valid, the function will return the decoded payload containing user information.

In addition to using JWT, another common technique for authentication in Node.js is the use of sessions. Sessions allow you to store user information on the server and associate it with a unique session token that is sent to the client for user identification. To use sessions in Node.js, you can use the 'express-session' library.

Here is an example of how you can use sessions with 'express-session' in Node.js:

```javascript
const express = require('express');
const session = require('express-session');

const app = express();
```

```
app.use(session({
  secret: 'mysecretkey',
  resave: false,
  saveUninitialized: false
}));

app.get('/', (req, res) => {
  req.session.user = {
    id: 123456,
    username: 'johndoe'
  };

  res.send('Session created');
});

app.get('/profile', (req, res) => {
```

```
    if (req.session.user) {

    res.send(`Welcome, ${req.session.user.username}`);

    } else {

    res.send('User not authenticated');

    }
});


app.listen(3000, () => {

    console.log('Server started on port 3000');

});
```

In this example, the `session` function from 'express-session' is used to create a session with a secret key `mysecretkey`. The `req.session` object is used to store user information within the session. In the '/profile' route, it is checked if the user is authenticated by verifying the presence of the `req.session.user` object.

Once a robust authentication system is implemented, it is crucial to also consider user authorization within the application. This can be done by using custom middleware to verify user permissions before allowing access to certain resources or features.

Here is an example of how you can implement a custom authorization middleware in Node.js:

```javascript
const checkPermissions = (req, res, next) => {
  if (req.session.user && req.session.user.role === 'admin') {
    next();
  } else {
    res.status(403).send('Access denied');
  }
```

```
};

app.get('/admin', checkPermissions, (req, res) => {
  res.send('Administration panel');
});
```

In this example, the `checkPermissions` middleware is used to check if the user has an admin role before allowing access to the '/admin' route. If the user is not authorized, the middleware will return a 403 status (Access denied).

In addition to creating custom middleware, you can also use authorization libraries like 'casbin' or 'express-jwt-permissions' to simplify the management of permissions in Node.js. These libraries allow you to define authorization rules based on roles or permissions and apply them easily and effectively within the application.

Managing permissions and authentications in Node.js is a critical aspect to ensure the security of web applications. By using techniques like using JWT, sessions, and custom middleware, you can implement a robust and secure authentication and authorization system to protect the resources of the application and ensure that only authorized users can access certain features or sensitive data.

14. Deploying a Node.js application

Managing permissions and authentication in Node.js is a fundamental aspect to ensure the security of web applications. In this article, we will explore different techniques and libraries that can be used to implement a robust and secure authentication and authorization system in a Node.js application.

Authentication is the process by which a user proves to be who they say they are, while authorization is the process by which it is determined which actions a user is authorized to perform within the application. These two aspects are crucial to protect the application's resources and ensure that only authorized users can access specific functionalities or sensitive data.

One of the most common techniques for authentication in Node.js is using JSON Web Tokens (JWT). A JWT is a digitally signed token that contains user information and can be used to verify the authenticity of a user. To use JWT in Node.js, you can use the `jsonwebtoken` library.

Here's an example of how you can generate a JWT in Node.js:

```javascript
const jwt = require('jsonwebtoken');

const payload = {
  user_id: 123456,
  username: 'johndoe'
};

const secretKey = 'mysecretkey';
```

```javascript
const token = jwt.sign(payload, secretKey, { expiresIn: '1h' });

console.log(token);
```

In this example, the `jwt.sign` function is used to generate a JWT from a payload containing user information. The generated token has a duration of 1 hour and is signed using the secret key `mysecretkey`.

Once the JWT is generated, you can use it to authenticate the user in subsequent requests by sending the token in the authorization headers. Here's an example of how you can verify a JWT in Node.js:

```javascript
const jwt = require('jsonwebtoken');
```

```
const secretKey = 'mysecretkey';
const token = 'xxxxxxxxxxxxxxxxxxxxxxxxxxxxxx'; // JWT to verify

jwt.verify(token, secretKey, (err, decoded) => {
  if (err) {
    console.error('Invalid token');
  } else {
    console.log(decoded);
  }
});
```
```

In this example, the `jwt.verify` function is used to verify a JWT using the secret key `mysecretkey`. If the token is valid, the
```

function will return the decoded payload containing user information.

In addition to using JWT, another common technique for authentication in Node.js is using sessions. Sessions allow you to store user information on the server and associate it with a unique session token that is sent to the client for user identification. To use sessions in Node.js, you can use the `express-session` library.

Here's an example of how you can use sessions with `express-session` in Node.js:

```javascript
const express = require('express');
const session = require('express-session');

const app = express();
```

```javascript
app.use(session({
  secret: 'mysecretkey',
  resave: false,
  saveUninitialized: false
}));

app.get('/', (req, res) => {
  req.session.user = {
    id: 123456,
    username: 'johndoe'
  };

  res.send('Session created');
});

app.get('/profile', (req, res) => {
```

```
  if (req.session.user) {

    res.send(`Welcome, ${req.session.user.username}`);

  } else {

    res.send('User not authenticated');

  }
});


app.listen(3000, () => {

  console.log('Server started on port 3000');

});
```

In this example, the `session` function of `express-session` is used to create a session with a secret key `mysecretkey`. The `req.session` object is used to store user information within the session. In the `/profile` route, it is checked if the user is authenticated by checking the existence of the `req.session.user` object.

Once a robust authentication system is implemented, it is essential to also consider user authorization within the application. This can be done by using custom middleware to check user permissions before allowing access to specific resources or functionalities.

Here's an example of how you can implement a custom authorization middleware in Node.js:

```javascript
const checkPermissions = (req, res, next) => {
  if (req.session.user && req.session.user.role === 'admin') {
    next();
  } else {
    res.status(403).send('Access denied');
  }
```

```
};

app.get('/admin', checkPermissions, (req, res) => {
  res.send('Administration panel');
});
```

In this example, the `checkPermissions` middleware is used to check if the user has the administrator role before allowing access to the `/admin` route. If the user is not authorized, the middleware will return a 403 status (Access denied).

In addition to creating custom middleware, you can also use authorization libraries like `casbin` or `express-jwt-permissions` to simplify authorization management in Node.js. These libraries allow you to define authorization rules based on roles or permissions and apply them effectively within the application.

Managing permissions and authentication in Node.js is a critical aspect to ensure the security of web applications. By using techniques such as JWT, sessions, and custom middleware, you can implement a robust and secure authentication and authorization system to protect the application's resources and ensure that only authorized users can access specific functionalities or sensitive data.

15. Testing and Debugging in Node.js

Testing and debugging are fundamental practices in the development of any software application, including Node.js applications. In this article, we will delve into the concept of testing and debugging in Node.js, providing practical examples to demonstrate how to do it effectively.

Testing in Node.js:

Testing is an essential process to ensure that the developed code functions correctly and meets the specified requirements. There are different types of tests that can be performed on Node.js code, including unit tests, integration tests, and end-to-end tests.

One of the most popular testing frameworks for Node.js is Mocha. Mocha is a flexible and feature-rich testing framework that allows you to write and execute tests simply and efficiently. Below is an example of how to use Mocha to run a unit test on a simple function in Node.js.

Let's say we have an `add` function that takes two numbers as arguments and returns the sum of the two numbers:

```javascript
function add(a, b) {
  return a + b;
}
```

To test this function with Mocha, we could write a test like this:

```javascript
const assert = require('assert');
```

```
describe('add', function() {

  it('should return the sum of two numbers', function() {

    assert.equal(add(1, 2), 3);

  });

});
```

In this example, we are using the `describe` method to define a test group and the `it` method to define a single test within that group. We are also using the `assert` module from Node.js to verify that the result of the `add` function is correct.

Once the test is written, you can run it using the `mocha` command on the command line. Mocha will run the test and provide a detailed report of the results, including tests that passed and tests that failed.

In addition to Mocha, there are other popular testing frameworks for Node.js, such as Jest and Jasmine. These frameworks offer additional features and are used for unit tests, integration tests, and end-to-end tests.

Debugging in Node.js:

Debugging is the process of identifying and fixing errors in the source code. The Node.js debugger provides powerful tools for finding and resolving bugs in Node.js code, allowing developers to step through the code and observe variable values at each stage of execution.

Node.js includes a built-in debugger that can be activated using the `inspect` flag at runtime. For example, you can run a Node.js application in debug mode using the following command:

```bash
```

```
node --inspect app.js
```

Once the debugger is started, you can connect to it using the Chrome browser by entering `chrome://inspect` in the browser's address bar. From here, you can inspect the code, set breakpoints, and step through the code to identify and resolve bugs.

In addition to the built-in debugger, there are third-party tools that offer advanced debugging features for Node.js. For example, the Node.js framework Visual Studio Code includes a built-in debugger that allows you to debug Node.js code directly within the editor.

Example of debugging with Visual Studio Code:

Let's say we have a `multiply` function that takes two numbers as arguments and returns the product of the two numbers:

```javascript
function multiply(a, b) {
  return a * b;
}

const result = multiply(2, 3);
console.log(result);
```

If we run this code in Visual Studio Code and activate the debugger, we can set a breakpoint on the `console.log(result)` line and step through the code to observe variable values and identify any errors in the code.

The Visual Studio Code debugger allows you to follow the code execution flow, view variable values, and check the program's state at any point during execution. This tool is extremely useful for identifying and resolving complex bugs in Node.js code.

In conclusion, testing and debugging are essential practices to ensure that Node.js code functions correctly and meets the specified requirements. By using testing frameworks like Mocha and debuggers like Visual Studio Code, you can effectively identify and resolve bugs, improving the quality and reliability of software developed with Node.js.

16. Scalability and load balancing in Node.js

Scalability and load balancing are two fundamental concepts when it comes to handling large amounts of traffic and requests on a Node.js-based web application. In this article, we will delve into how to implement a scalable and efficient solution using the server-side JavaScript framework.

Node.js is known for its ability to efficiently handle a large number of simultaneous connections due to its event-driven asynchronous I/O model. However, when the number of requests significantly increases, it may be necessary to use multiple instances of the Node.js server to distribute the load and ensure optimal performance.

One of the most common ways to scale a Node.js application is to use a load balancing system that distributes traffic across multiple servers. The load balancer can be implemented at the software or hardware level and can be configured to distribute requests based on various criteria, such as workload or available resources.

An example of a very popular software load balancing solution is Nginx, a lightweight, high-performance proxy server and load balancer. Nginx can be configured to serve as a front-end for multiple instances of a Node.js application behind it, evenly distributing requests among the various servers.

Suppose we have a Node.js application that handles a large number of RESTful requests from different clients. In this case, we can configure Nginx to distribute traffic among multiple instances of Node.js on the same server or on different servers, ensuring better load balancing and greater scalability.

Another common strategy to scale a Node.js

application is to use clustering, which allows creating multiple Node.js processes sharing the same listening port. Clustering enables leveraging server multi-cores to handle multiple concurrent requests more efficiently.

For example, we can use the `cluster` module of Node.js to create a cluster of processes listening on the same port. This way, each request is automatically distributed among the active processes, ensuring better load management and greater scalability.

Here is an example of how to create a Node.js process cluster using the `cluster` module:

```javascript
const cluster = require('cluster');

const os = require('os');


if (cluster.isMaster) {
```

```javascript
// Get the number of CPU cores
const numCPUs = os.cpus().length;

// Fork a new process for each CPU core
for (let i = 0; i < numCPUs; i++) {
  cluster.fork();
}

// Handle process death and fork a new process
cluster.on('exit', (worker, code, signal) => {
  console.log(`Worker ${worker.process.pid} died, restarting...`);
  cluster.fork();
});
} else {
// Start the Node.js server in each worker process
```

```
  require('./app');
}
```

In this example, the main process creates a cluster of Node.js processes corresponding to the server's CPU cores. Each process listens on the same port, and requests are evenly distributed among the processes by the operating system.

Lastly, another approach to scale a Node.js application is to use a cloud hosting service like Amazon Web Services (AWS) or Google Cloud Platform (GCP). These services offer scalable and managed services like AWS Elastic Beanstalk or GCP App Engine, which make it easy to deploy and manage multiple instances of a Node.js application automatically and transparently.

Scalability and load balancing are crucial to

ensuring optimal performance of a Node.js application capable of handling a large volume of traffic and concurrent requests. By using solutions such as process clustering, load balancing with Nginx, or scalable cloud services, it is possible to ensure greater efficiency and reliability of the system.

17. Best practices and tips for development with Node.js: Polly, custom long-polling with node.js

Node.js is a JavaScript runtime that allows you to run server-side JavaScript code. It is a powerful tool for web application development and, if used correctly, can offer exceptional performance. In this article, we will discuss best practices and tips for development with Node.js, particularly for implementing Polly, a custom long-polling technique.

Before getting started, it is important to understand what Polly is and how it works. Polly is a long-polling technique that allows you to keep an open connection between the client and server to receive real-time updates. It is particularly useful for real-time applications that require constant updates without manual page refreshes. With Node.js, you can implement a custom long-polling solution that fits the specific needs of your application.

Here are some best practices and tips for development with Node.js and implementing Polly with examples:

1. Use npm modules:

Node.js has a vast ecosystem of npm modules that allow you to extend the basic runtime functionalities. Before implementing Polly, make sure to look for npm modules that can streamline the development process. For example, you can use modules like express for HTTP route handling or socket.io for real-time communication between client and server.

2. Handle exceptions properly:

Node.js uses asynchronous programming as its model, meaning operations are executed non-sequentially. It is important to handle exceptions properly to prevent the server from crashing in case of errors or unhandled exceptions. Make sure to use try-catch blocks or utilize Express's error handling method to catch any exceptions.

3. Perform input parameter validation:

When receiving data from the client, it is important to validate input parameters to prevent injection attacks or validation errors. Use modules like body-parser to parse data sent from HTTP requests and implement checks to verify that the data is in the correct format and adheres to the validation rules defined by your application.

4. Use WebSocket for bidirectional communication:

If you are implementing a long-polling solution to allow real-time communication between client and server, you may want to consider using WebSocket instead of long-polling. WebSocket is a bidirectional communication protocol that allows for more efficient and instantaneous communication compared to long-polling. Socket.io is a Node.js framework that simplifies the implementation of WebSocket and provides additional features like automatic connection handling and automatic reconnection.

5. Implement a timeout mechanism:

It is important to implement a timeout mechanism to prevent long-polling connections from remaining open indefinitely. Define a maximum timeout for long-polling requests and close the connection if you do not receive updates within the specified timeout. This way, you will avoid server overload and ensure resources are used efficiently.

6. Use Redis for short-term storage:

If your application requires temporary data storage to provide real-time updates through long-polling technique, you may want to consider using Redis as a short-term storage server. Redis is an in-memory database that offers high-speed access and a wide range of data structures that can be used to store real-time updates and exchange them between client and server.

Here is an example of how to implement Polly with Node.js using Express and WebSocket:

```
// Import necessary modules
const express = require('express');
const http = require('http');
const WebSocket = require('ws');

// Create an Express app and an HTTP server
const app = express();
const server = http.createServer(app);
```

```javascript
// Create a WebSocket server and listen for connections
const wss = new WebSocket.Server({ server });

wss.on('connection', function connection(ws) {
  // When a client connects, send a confirmation message
  ws.send('Connection established successfully');

  // Simulate sending real-time updates every 5 seconds
  setInterval(() => {
    ws.send('Real-time update');
  }, 5000);
});
```

```
// Start the HTTP server
server.listen(3000, function() {
  console.log('Server listening on port 3000');
});
```

This is just an example of how to implement Polly with Node.js using Express and WebSocket. You can customize and adapt this code to the specific needs of your application to ensure effective real-time communication between client and server.

Development with Node.js offers a wide variety of tools and modules that can be used to implement advanced solutions like Polly for real-time communication. By following the best practices and tips suggested in this article, you can create performant and scalable web applications that provide an exceptional user experience.

18. WebSocket and Node.js

WebSocket is a communication protocol that provides a bidirectional connection between a server and a client through a low-latency, low-overhead communication channel. This allows servers to send messages to clients and vice versa in real-time, without the need for continuous page refresh or creating new HTTP connections for each request.

Node.js is a JavaScript runtime based on the Google Chrome V8 JavaScript engine, which allows running server-side JavaScript code and interacting with the operating system to perform non-blocking, asynchronous I/O operations. Node.js is particularly suitable for creating scalable, high-performance web applications, thanks to its event-driven architecture and ability to handle a large number of concurrent connections.

When WebSocket and Node.js are combined,

it is possible to create highly performant real-time web applications, such as real-time chats, online games, sensor monitoring, and much more. In this article, we will see how to implement a WebSocket server in Node.js and create a WebSocket client to interact with it.

To get started, we need to install the 'ws' module for Node.js, which allows us to create the WebSocket server. We can do this using npm with the following command:

```
npm install ws
```

Once the 'ws' module is installed, we can start creating our WebSocket server. Here is an example of how to create a WebSocket server in Node.js:

```javascript
const WebSocket = require('ws');

const wss = new WebSocket.Server({ port: 8080 });

wss.on('connection', function connection(ws) {
  console.log('New client connected');

  ws.on('message', function incoming(message) {
    console.log('Received: %s', message);
    ws.send('Message received');
  });

  ws.on('close', function close() {
    console.log('Client disconnected');
```

```
  });
});
```

In this code, we create a WebSocket server that listens on port 8080 and handles client connections. When a client connects, the server sends a log message and listens for client messages. When a client sends a message, the server receives it, sends a log message, and responds with a confirmation message. When the client disconnects, the server sends a log message.

Once the WebSocket server is created, we can create a WebSocket client to interact with it. Here is an example of how to create a WebSocket client in Node.js:

```javascript
const WebSocket = require('ws');
```

```
const ws = new WebSocket('ws://localhost:8080');

ws.on('open', function open() {
  console.log('Connected to server');
  ws.send('Hello, server');
});

ws.on('message', function incoming(data) {
  console.log('Received: %s', data);
});

ws.on('close', function close() {
  console.log('Disconnected from server');
});
```

In this example, we create a WebSocket client that connects to the WebSocket server listening on port 8080. When the client connects, it sends a log message and a message to the server. When the server responds with a message, the client receives it and sends a log message. When the server disconnects, the client receives a log message.

In summary, WebSocket and Node.js are a powerful combination for creating highly performant real-time web applications. By using the 'ws' module of Node.js, it is easy to create both a WebSocket server and a WebSocket client to interact in real-time through a bidirectional connection. Thanks to their event-driven architecture and support for asynchronous connections, WebSocket and Node.js allow for creating scalable, high-performance web applications.

19. Example of a real-time application with WebSocket and Node.js

Let's create a real-time application using WebSocket and Node.js. WebSocket is a technology that enables bidirectional communication between the server and the client in real-time. Node.js is a server-side JavaScript runtime that allows you to run JavaScript code on the server side.

First, let's create a folder for the project and initialize a Node.js project using the command npm init. Next, let's install the websocket package using the command npm install websocket.

```javascript
// server.js

const WebSocket = require('ws');
```

```javascript
const wss = new WebSocket.Server({ port: 3000 });

wss.on('connection', function connection(ws) {
  console.log('Client connected');

  ws.on('message', function incoming(message) {
    console.log('Received: %s', message);
    // Send the message to all clients except the one who sent it
    wss.clients.forEach(function each(client) {
      if (client !== ws && client.readyState === WebSocket.OPEN) {
        client.send(message);
      }
    });
```

```javascript
  });

  ws.on('close', function close() {
    console.log('Client disconnected');
  });
});
```

This is our Node.js server that handles the WebSocket connection. We use the ws package to create a WebSocket server on port 3000. When a client connects, we send a log message and register the 'message' and 'close' events. When a client sends a message, we forward it to all connected clients except the sender.

```javascript
// client.html
```

```html
<!DOCTYPE html>
<html lang="en">
<head>
  <meta charset="UTF-8">
  <meta name="viewport" content="width=device-width, initial-scale=1.0">
  <title>WebSocket Client</title>
</head>
<body>
  <input type="text" id="message" placeholder="Type a message">
  <button onclick="sendMessage()">Send</button>
  <div id="chat"></div>

  <script>
    const ws = new WebSocket('ws://localhost:3000');
```

```javascript
const chat = document.getElementById('chat');

ws.onmessage = function(event) {
    const message = document.createElement('p');
    message.textContent = event.data;
    chat.appendChild(message);
};

function sendMessage() {
    const input = document.getElementById('message');
    const message = input.value;
    ws.send(message);
    input.value = '';
}
</script>
```

```
</body>
</html>
```

This is our HTML client that connects to the WebSocket server on port 3000. We use the WebSocket object to send and receive messages from the server. When the client receives a message, we display it in the div with id 'chat'. When the user writes a message and clicks the 'Send' button, we send the message to the server.

This is how you can create a real-time application using WebSocket and Node.js. The server handles communication between clients and forwards messages in real-time to all connected clients. The client interacts with the server by sending and receiving messages via WebSocket.

20. Monitoring and logging in Node.js

Monitoring and logging are essential to ensure the proper functioning of a Node.js application in production. In this article, we will see how to implement an effective monitoring and logging system using various libraries and tools available in the Node.js ecosystem.

Introduction to monitoring and logging in Node.js

When developing a Node.js application, it is important to track performance and the state of the application in real-time. Monitoring allows to identify any issues and intervene promptly to resolve them. Logging, on the other hand, is useful for recording detailed information about the application's execution, useful for understanding its behavior and resolving any bugs.

Node.js offers various libraries and tools to implement monitoring and logging effectively. In this article, we will see how to use some of these libraries and tools to implement a complete and efficient monitoring and logging system.

Implementation of monitoring in Node.js

To implement monitoring in Node.js, we can use various libraries and tools. Among the most popular ones are:

- New Relic: New Relic is a real-time application monitoring tool that offers a comprehensive overview of the application's performance and state. To use New Relic with Node.js, simply install the newrelic module via npm and configure the license key obtained from the official New Relic website.

- PM2: PM2 is a Node.js process manager that offers advanced process monitoring and management features. To use PM2 with Node.js, simply install the pm2 module via npm and start the application using the pm2 start command.

- Prometheus: Prometheus is an open-source monitoring and alerting system that offers support for Node.js through the prom-client module. To use Prometheus with Node.js, install the prom-client module via npm and configure the Prometheus server to collect the application's metric data.

Implementation of logging in Node.js

To implement logging in Node.js, we can use various libraries and tools. Among the most popular ones are:

- Winston: Winston is a flexible and customizable logging library that supports different log levels and outputs. To use Winston with Node.js, install the winston module via npm and configure the desired output transports (console, file, database, etc.).

- Bunyan: Bunyan is a fast and efficient logging library that supports log formatting and stream management. To use Bunyan with Node.js, install the bunyan module via npm and configure the logger with the desired output transports.

- Log4js: Log4js is a flexible and configurable logging library that supports log file rotation and log levels management. To use Log4js with Node.js, install the log4js module via npm and configure the logger with the desired output transports.

Conclusions

Monitoring and logging are essential to ensure the proper functioning of a Node.js application in production. In this article, we have seen how to implement an effective monitoring and logging system using various libraries and tools available in the Node.js ecosystem. With a proper monitoring and logging system, it is possible to promptly identify any issues and intervene promptly to resolve them, ensuring the reliability and performance of the application.

Index

1. Introduction to Node.js pg.4

2. Installation of Node.js pg.7

3. JavaScript Fundamentals in Node.js pg.17

4. Modules and Packages in Node.js pg.31

5. Error Handling in Node.js pg.48

6. Events and callbacks in Node.js pg.58

7. Creating a web server with Node.js pg.67

8. Managing HTTP requests with Node.js (GET and POST) HTML Template for Node.js pg.75

9. Creating APIs with Node.js pg.84

10. Database Connectivity with Node.js pg.96

11. Using middleware in Node.js pg.105

12. Session and Cookie Management in Node.js pg.111

13. Authorization and authentication management in Node.js pg.120

14. Deploying a Node.js application pg.130

15. Testing and Debugging in Node.js pg.140

16. Scalability and load balancing in Node.js pg.147

17. Best practices and tips for development with Node.js: Polly, custom long-polling with node.js pg.153

18. WebSocket and Node.js pg.160

19. Example of a real-time application with WebSocket and Node.js pg.166

20. Monitoring and logging in Node.js pg.172

www.ingramcontent.com/pod-product-compliance
Lightning Source LLC
Chambersburg PA
CBHW050058230526
45470CB00004B/1583